Butterflies

by Martha London

FOCUS
READERS.

PIONEER

www.focusreaders.com

Focus Readers is distributed by North Star Editions:
sales@northstareditions.com | 888-417-0195

Produced for Focus Readers by Red Line Editorial.

Photographs ©: Shutterstock Images, cover, 1, 4, 7, 8, 11, 13, 14, 17, 18, 21 (chrysalis); Red Line Editorial, 21 (chart)

Library of Congress Cataloging-in-Publication Data
Names: London, Martha, author.
Title: Butterflies / by Martha London.
Description: Lake Elmo, MN : Focus Readers, [2021] | Series: Neighborhood safari | Includes index. | Audience: Grades 2-3
Identifiers: LCCN 2019060237 (print) | LCCN 2019060238 (ebook) | ISBN 9781644933527 (hardcover) | ISBN 9781644934289 (paperback) | ISBN 9781644935804 (pdf) | ISBN 9781644935040 (ebook)
Subjects: LCSH: Butterflies--Juvenile literature.
Classification: LCC QL544.2 .L69 2021 (print) | LCC QL544.2 (ebook) | DDC 595.78/9--dc23
LC record available at https://lccn.loc.gov/2019060237
LC ebook record available at https://lccn.loc.gov/2019060238

Printed in the United States of America
Mankato, MN
082020

About the Author

Martha London writes books for young readers. When she's not writing, you can find her hiking in the woods.

Table of Contents

Chapter 1

Bright Wings

A butterfly lands on an orange flower. Its colorful wings brush the petals. The butterfly sips the flower's **nectar**. Then it flaps its wings and flies away.

Butterflies are insects. There are more than 17,000 kinds of butterflies. Many live in warm places. Butterflies cannot fly when it is too cold. They get food from flowers. They are often found in gardens.

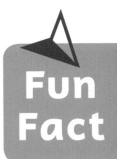

Fun Fact

A group of butterflies is called a kaleidoscope.

Chapter 2

Butterfly Bodies

A butterfly has six legs. It has two **antennae** on its head. The antennae help the butterfly sense its surroundings.

A butterfly's tongue is called a proboscis. It curls up under the butterfly's head.

A butterfly has four wings. They are covered in tiny scales. The scales come in many colors. Some are bright. Others are brown or black.

wing

antenna

eye

proboscis

body

leg

Copying Colors

Monarch butterflies are orange and black. Monarch **caterpillars** eat milkweed. This plant is poisonous. Animals that eat monarchs will get sick. The monarchs' colors tell **predators** to stay away.

Some butterflies trick predators. They look similar to monarchs. But they are not poisonous.

Chapter 3

Finding Flowers

Butterflies use their eyesight to find flowers. Bright colors **attract** butterflies. They look for flowers that are red, orange, or yellow.

Butterflies drink nectar from flowers. A butterfly lands on a flower's petals. It sticks its tongue inside. The tongue is long. It reaches deep into the flower. Butterflies lay eggs on plants, too.

Fun Fact

Butterflies taste with their feet.

Chapter 4

Migrating

Some kinds of butterflies **migrate**. They travel long distances during spring and fall. They often fly to places with **blooming** flowers. Monarch butterflies are one example.

Monarchs fly north from Mexico in the spring. They land in the United States and Canada. The butterflies lay eggs in these places. Caterpillars hatch. New butterflies fly back to Mexico in the fall.

Fun Fact

Millions of butterflies may land in the same place.

Life Cycle

Female butterflies lay eggs.

Caterpillars hatch from the eggs.

The caterpillars eat and grow.

Each caterpillar forms a hard shell.

An adult butterfly comes out of the shell.

Most butterflies live a few weeks.

FOCUS ON
Butterflies

Write your answers on a separate piece of paper.

1. Write a sentence explaining why butterflies live near flowers.

2. Would you like to travel thousands of miles every year? Why or why not?

3. What is the name for a butterfly's tongue?
   - A. caterpillar
   - B. proboscis
   - C. antenna

4. What might happen if butterflies did not migrate?
   - A. They might have more food to eat.
   - B. They might get too cold or run out of food.
   - C. They might blow away in the wind.

Answer key on page 24.

Glossary

antennae
Long, thin body parts on an insect's head that are used for sensing.

attract
To make something come closer.

blooming
Having open petals.

caterpillars
Young butterflies or moths that look similar to worms.

migrate
To move from one place to another when the seasons change.

nectar
A sweet liquid made by plants.

predators
Animals that hunt other animals for food.

To Learn More

BOOKS

McAneney, Caitie. *Butterflies Up Close*. New York: PowerKids Press, 2020.

York, M. J. *Butterflies and Moths*. Mankato, MN: The Child's World, 2020.

NOTE TO EDUCATORS

Visit **www.focusreaders.com** to find lesson plans, activities, links, and other resources related to this title.

Index

Answer Key: 1. Answers will vary; **2.** Answers will vary; **3.** B; **4.** B